Be grateful. Be mindful. Every day.

It will help you achieve your highest self.

S M T W TH F S   DATE: TIME:

S M T W TH F S   DATE: TIME:

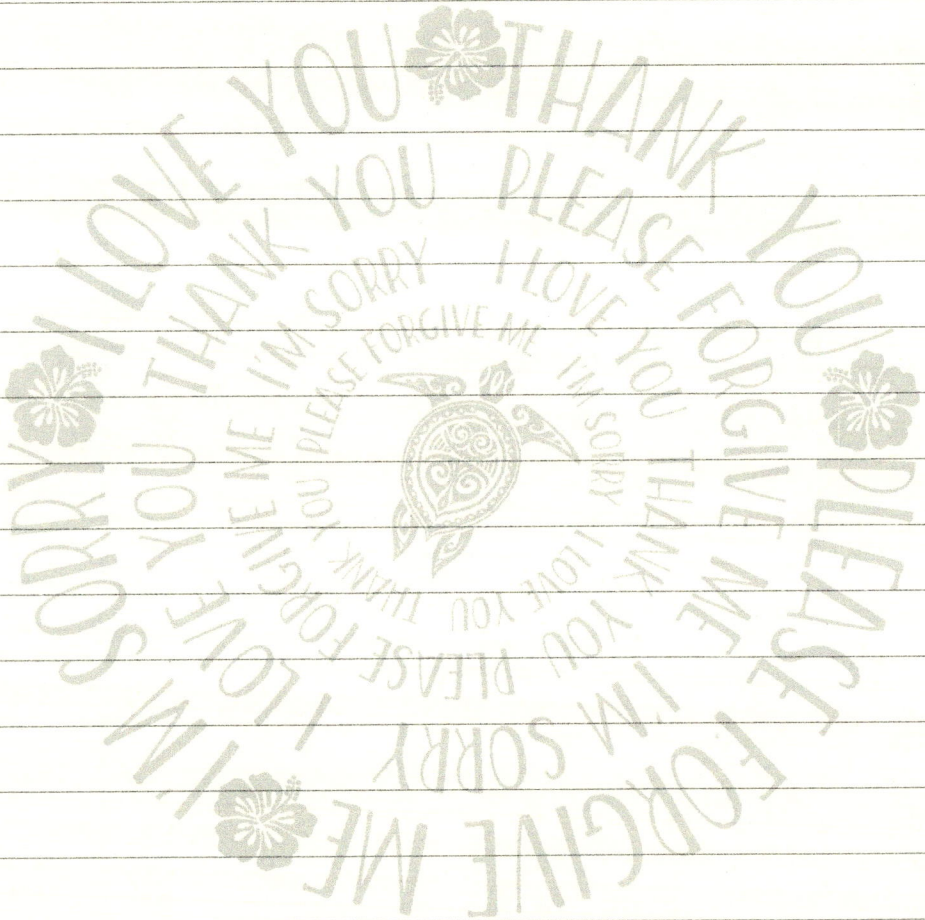

S M T W TH F S   DATE: TIME:

S   M   T   W   TH   F   S   DATE: TIME:

S M T W TH F S   DATE: TIME:

S M T W TH F S   DATE: TIME:

S M T W TH F S   DATE: TIME:

Made in the USA
Las Vegas, NV
19 December 2024